DATE DUE

Character Values

I Am
Patriotic

by Sarah L. Schuette

Consulting Editor: Gail Saunders-Smith, PhD
Consultant: Madonna Murphy, PhD
Professor of Education, University of St. Francis, Joliet, Illinois
Author, *Character Education in America's Blue Ribbon Schools*

Capstone
press

Mankato, Minnesota

Pebble Books are published by Capstone Press
151 Good Counsel Drive, P.O. Box 669, Mankato, Minnesota 56002
www.capstonepress.com

1 2 3 4 5 6 09 08 07 06 05 04

Library of Congress Cataloging-in-Publication Data
Schuette, Sarah L., 1976–
    I am patriotic / by Sarah L. Schuette.
    p. cm.—(Character values)
    Includes bibliographical references and index.
    ISBN 0-7368-2571-1 (hardcover)
    1. Patriotism—United States—Juvenile literature. [1. Patriotism.] I. Title.
II. Series.
JK1759.S335 2004
323.6'5'0973—dc22
                                            2003024150

Summary: Simple text and photographs illustrate how children can be patriotic.

Note to Parents and Teachers

The Character Values series supports national social studies standards for units on individual development and identity. This book describes the character value of patriotism and illustrates ways students can be patriotic. The images support early readers in understanding the text. The repetition of words and phrases helps early readers learn new words. This book also introduces early readers to subject-specific vocabulary words, which are defined in the Glossary. Early readers may need assistance to read some words and to use the Table of Contents, Glossary, Read More, Internet Sites, and Index/Word List sections of the book.

Table of Contents

Being Patriotic

I am patriotic. I am proud of my country.

I help my parents
hang a flag.

Patriotism at School

I learn about
patriotic people.

My class writes letters to soldiers. We tell them that we are proud of them.

U. S. POST OFFICE

In the Community

I respect government buildings and workers.

I visit a museum. I learn about people who helped my country.

I thank veterans for helping our country.

I learn to say the Pledge of Allegiance.

I am patriotic. I celebrate my country.

Glossary

celebrate—to do something fun on a special occasion

museum—a place where visitors can see historical objects and art

patriotic—loyal to a country

Pledge of Allegiance—a promise to be loyal to the United States and its flag

respect—a belief in the quality and worth of yourself, others, ideas, and customs; respectful people treat others the way they would like to be treated.

veteran—someone who has served in the military

Read More

DeFord, Deborah H. *Patriotism.* Character Education. Chicago: Raintree, 2003.

Raatma, Lucia. *Patriotism.* Character Education. Mankato, Minn.: Bridgestone Books, 2000.

Scheunemann, Pam. *Patriotism.* United We Stand. Edina, Minn.: Abdo, 2003.

Internet Sites

FactHound offers a safe, fun way to find Internet sites related to this book. All of the sites on FactHound have been researched by our staff.

Here's how:

1. Visit *www.facthound.com*
2. Type in this special code **0736825711** for age-appropriate sites. Or enter a search word related to this book for a more general search.
3. Click on the **Fetch It** button.

FactHound will fetch the best sites for you!

Index/Word List

Word Count: 76
Early-Intervention Level: 13

Editorial Credits

Mari C. Schuh, editor; Jennifer Bergstrom, series designer and illustrator; Enoch Peterson, book designer; Karen Hieb, product planning editor

Photo Credits

All photos by Capstone Press/Gem Photo Studio/Dan Delaney, except page 20 (background), Corel

The author dedicates this book to her aunt Ruth and uncle Frank Hilgers, of Belle Plaine, Minnesota.